THE NATIONAL POETRY SERIES

Ninth Annual Series–1988

Jeffrey Harrison, *The Singing Underneath*
(Selected by James Merrill)

Marie Howe, *The Good Thief*
(Selected by Margaret Atwood)

William Olsen, *The Hand of God and a Few Bright Flowers*
(Selected by David Wagoner)

Jeffrey Skinner, *A Guide to Forgetting*
(Selected by Tess Gallagher)

Leigh Cole Swensen, *New Math*
(Selected by Michael Palmer)

The National Poetry Series was established in 1978 to publish five collections of poetry annually through participating publishers. The manuscripts are selected by five poets of national reputation. Publication is funded by the Copernicus Society of America, James A. Michener, Edward J. Piszek, the Mobil Foundation, The National Endowment for the Arts, the Friends of the National Poetry Series, and the five publishers—E. P. Dutton, Graywolf Press, William Morrow & Co., Persea Books, and the University of Illinois Press.

The Singing
Underneath

Jeffrey Harrison

The Singing Underneath

The National Poetry Series   *Selected by James Merrill*

E. P. DUTTON NEW YORK

☐ Published in the United States by E. P. Dutton, a division of NAL Penguin Inc., 2 Park Avenue, New York, N.Y. 10016. ☐ Published simultaneously in Canada by Fitzhenry and Whiteside, Limited, Toronto. ☐ Library of Congress Cataloging-in-Publication Data: Harrison, Jeffrey. ☐ The singing underneath / Jeffrey Harrison; selected by James Merrill. ☐ p. cm. — (The National poetry series) ☐ ISBN 0-525-24640-1. ISBN 0-525-48383-7 (pbk.) ☐ I. Merrill, James Ingram. II. Title. III. Series. ☐ PS3558.A67133S5 1988 ☐ 811'.54— dc19 ☐ Designed by Earl Tidwell ☐ 1 2 3 4 5 6 7 8 9 10 ☐ First Edition

Some of the poems in this volume appeared, sometimes in slightly different form, in the following periodicals:

The Antioch Review: "How the Ginkgo Got Its Smell"
Boulevard: "Elegy for the Clotheslines," "In Saint John the Divine"
Crazyhorse: "Skating in Late Afternoon"
Harvard Magazine: "Field and Woods"
The Hudson Review: "In the Attic"
Margin: "Scallop," "The Singing Underneath"
The Missouri Review: "Arrival at the Cabin," "Butterflies," "For a Friend in the Hospital," "Hornets' Nest," "The Peacock Flounder," "Poem," "Returning to Cuttyhunk"
The New Republic: "Canoeing with My Brother"
Ontario Review: "Slaughter Cows"
Poetry: "Bathtubs, Three Varieties," "The Hummingbird Feeder," "The One That Got Away"
The Quarterly: "Country Wedding," "The Model House," "Moth and Dragonfly: Two Memories," "The New Geography," "Shooting at the Sky"
Southwest Review: "Trading the Alps for the Andes"
Verse: "A Field Guide to Mosses"
Willow Springs: "The Mute Swan"
The Yale Review: "Reflection on the Vietnam War Memorial"

"Butterflies" was reprinted in the *Arvon Foundation International Poetry Competition 1985 Anthology* (Arvon Foundation, 1987).
"The Hummingbird Feeder" was reprinted in *The Anthology of Magazine Verse and Yearbook of American Poetry* (Monitor Book Company, Inc., 1985).
"In the Attic" was reprinted in *The Anthology of Magazine Verse and Yearbook of American Poetry* (Monitor Book Co., Inc., 1988).
Ten of the poems in this volume appeared in a chapbook, also called *The Singing Underneath,* published by Windhover Press (Iowa City, 1986).

For my parents
Anne Woods Harrison
and
Robert Sattler Harrison

ACKNOWLEDGMENTS

I would like to thank Stanford University and the Ohio Arts Council for fellowships which helped me to complete this book.

Special thanks to Peter Schmitt for suggestions and generous assistance.

CONTENTS

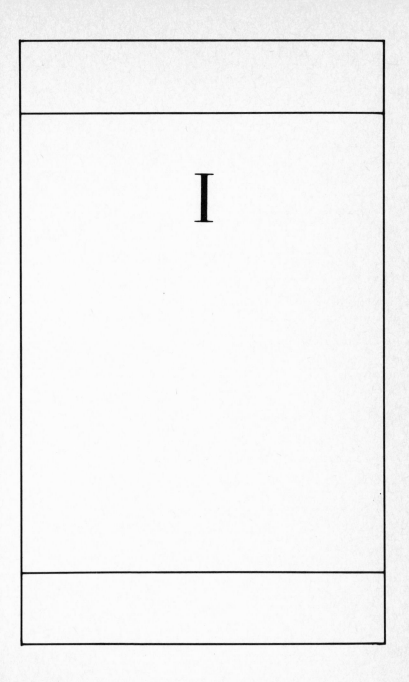

I

THE SINGING UNDERNEATH

The sun comes out, steam rises
from the field, and the ice-glazed trees
begin to drip. A few prismatic drops

quiver on the branches like tiny,
fidgeting birds. No, more like
a visual singing of birds: as if,

just underneath the world we see,
there is a silent singing that breaks out
at moments, in flickering points of light.

CANOEING WITH MY BROTHER

FOR JEREMY

A bullfrog's low reverberation
draws us toward the inkblot of the shore.
Nothing has changed since we were boys:
the beam of the flashlight in the mist
bounces off the water, up into the trees,
then spotlights him, a paddle's length away,

a Buddha on a heart-shaped lily pad.
Though he's been calling for a mate all night,
his eyes are absent of desire. The light
spreads through his limbs, paralyzing him,
except his throat, which pulses slightly.
His milky belly bulges against the leaf.

Years ago, we would have smacked him with a paddle
and later cut his legs off, peeling the skin
from braided flesh, like long green rubber gloves—
white and red-veined as they turned inside out
down to the tips of the long, bony toes.
These legs he would have died for

are folded into compact Z's. His arms
look atrophied, vestigial in contrast,
the hands turned inward like the hands
of an aikido master or someone
in a Japanese tea ceremony
"sitting seiza," just about to bow.

Another frog, nearby, starts bellowing.
"He'll never do it with us next to him,"
my brother whispers. But just then
his throat swells bigger than a chicken egg,
and with no change of expression,
with no expression at all, he starts to sing.

THE HUMMINGBIRD FEEDER

If what we wait to see partly defines us,
then this red bulb hanging in the blue
is a simple model for the heart,
swaying slightly at the end of its string
as I rock slightly, standing next to it,
eyes fixed, waiting for the buzz, the blur
of wings, the body like a tiny seal's
balancing the feeder on its nose.

Surely these moments we stand on tiptoe for
make us what we are as much as pain
and sorrow: the moment the hummingbird
flashes his red throat, the moment he spreads
his tail and swerves off like a fish, a green
streak, then sticks like a leaf to a branch—
the moment he stops in midair and sticks
his beak into that severed artery.

As he drinks, an embolism forms,
like the bubble in a spirit level,
and rises slowly up the tube, a bit
of the outside world going in, a moment
trapped: like one of those clear marbles
in which everything is upside-down, and small.
As the last drop quivers and disappears
with the bird, the heart becomes a mind.

HORNETS' NEST

I looked up and there it was,
like the light bulb of an idea:
a hornets' nest under the eaves
about the size of an onion.
And it grew like an onion, too,
in papery layers, each day
a little bigger, till it hung
like a thousand-year-old paper
lantern, parched and charred by time—

or like a weathered skull. I thought
of the combs inside, the tiers
of hexagonal cells (a pattern
infinitely extendible)
in which the larvae germinate
like seeds, or like ideas,
until the nest is bristling
with hornets, black- and yellow-striped
and buzzing like electrical sparks.

IN THE ATTIC

The thick air smelled of dust and wood.
Shiny, blue-black wasps, dangling their legs,
bounced off the facets of the roof
with quick, electrical buzzes.
I used to stay up there for hours, sitting
on the rough floor, jagged with splinters,

paging through stacks of *Life* magazine.
Or I'd stare through the Gothic window,
past spider webs, dead wasps,
and the ragged nests the starlings
had stuffed into the bargeboard, to feel
what it's like to be in the treetops.

This time I was up there for a reason.
Years ago, in the top drawer of a dresser
my mother had painted Pennsylvania Dutch,
I'd found a bundle of envelopes
stained amber by the attic's heat
like the mattresses piled on the old brass bed.

I'd been afraid to read them. Now,
I untied the dull blue ribbon.
It stayed crimped and folded from the bow.
The yellow pages crackled as I opened them.
They were written by my father, full of
ambition, jealousy, infatuation.

It was a side of him I'd never seen.
I had written letters like these
when I was fourteen, letters I'd burn
to see now. I read each one, one for every
day that summer. There was one from my mother:
blue ink on white paper, no envelope.

She described a view I knew by heart:
the lake framed by hemlocks, the mountain
reflected in the evening, its rock face
staring blankly. She said it made her think
of God. She said, yes, she would be his wife
if he was sure he understood what that meant.

COUNTRY WEDDING

After two days of rain, the sun
came out, miraculously, at four,
and the birds began to sing like crazy.

The guests assembled in the orchard
where a harp and flute were playing.
A rooster in the barnyard crowed

and the procession began:
squelching footsteps in the muddy aisle—
the maid of honor almost lost a shoe.

The music stopped. The minister intoned,
"We are gathered here to celebrate . . ."
Two swallows, glinting blue, performed

acrobatic feats above the scene,
fluttering together for a moment
like the doves on willowware.

A bedraggled English setter sniffed its way
up the aisle and sat down by the bride:
a symbol of faithfulness, perhaps,

or beauty, since its name was Belle.
The sun shone brighter for the vows,
two ducks flew overhead just as the bride

and bridegroom kneeled, and the rooster
crowed again on the word *truth*
from chapter thirteen of Corinthians.

Near the end, I heard a distant siren;
then the dogs began to bark,
the geese to honk, the ducks to quack.

Six buzzards circled overhead, the late sun
shining on their bladelike underwings,
then glided out of sight behind the hill.

SHOOTING AT THE SKY

I wanted to be like them, my father's friends
sitting around a trash barrel in blood-
stained hunting vests, drinking beer and joking,
cleaning doves that were still warm, the guts
and feathers on their hands. I'd ask my father
for a sip of beer. He always gave me one.

And soon I was like them, standing on the hill
with a shotgun, my brothers nearby,
each of us under one of the cedars
that our father said were grave markers
from when the plague had swept through Ohio.
("How long ago was that?" I asked. "Cut one down
and count the rings," my father said.)

We waited quietly, watching the sky,
mistaking insects that flew by our faces
for distant doves. I loved the smell
of empty shotgun shells, the smell of oil
on the gun, the gleaming tunnels
of the barrels, like long binoculars,
and the clicking of the safety catch.

We heard gunshots from the other fields,
and then the doves swerved over the treetops,
dodging our shots, their wings pumping
that single flute note through their bodies.
When I hit one, it closed its wings and fell
out of the group, arcing to the ground.

Or, wounded, it flapped down awkwardly,
spiraling, then running. I'd catch it.
One of the last times I went, I grabbed one
by the head, and my hand was suddenly
given the power of flight, flapping wildly,
until the head came off in my hand
and the bird flew into a thicket.

MOTH AND DRAGONFLY: TWO MEMORIES

1

When I found the cocoon, my heart
beat like the moth beginning to emerge.
The way it was struggling
to squeeze through that small, frayed hole
told me something was wrong, so I tore
the silky fabric and pulled it, quivering,
out. The front of its body was orange,
and hairy, like a buffalo, with an owl's face
and two feathery horns. Its wings were curled,
as limp as wilted irises.
I spread them in the grass—my hands
trembled at their size, and their pattern
glared at me, a primitive mask. It twitched.
I hurried toward the house. Inside,
my fingertips felt slippery and dry:
then I saw the fine gold powder, as if
from rubbing the gilt edge of a Bible.

2

I was wrapping a fish in wet ferns
when I noticed something on the bank:
a dragonfly clutching the carcass
of another insect, from which it had sucked
all the life. It was sluggish and barely moved
when I touched it. I thought it had been hurt
in the struggle and was going to die.
Then I realized it had just emerged
from that empty shell. It had crawled
up from the bottom of the river
onto the bank, clamped down on a stick,
split open its back, and pulled itself
out, exhausted. Then it had extended
its telescopic abdomen, pumping blood
into its iridescent wings, all the while
clenching the old skin like a victim—
an emblem of regret, or victory.

THREE BROTHERS IN THE SNOW

Winter has its pleasures.
—GÉRARD DE NERVAL

Snow immediately comes to mind—
those mornings our hearts leapt (and they still do)
when we looked out at another world, another
planet. We'd stumble out all bundled up
like astronauts, kicking through lunar dust
whose sparkles made you fall in dizzy pleasure,
then roll over and make a snow angel.
Or if it was pouring down you'd really feel
like someone walking on the moon, falling
upward, gravity releasing you.

And sleds that had been hanging all year long
unnoticed on the wall of the garage
came down: toboggans, Flexible Flyers
(their runners, orange with rust, would shine again!),
and flying saucers dented from rough landings.
No hill was too steep for us; we tried them all,
crashing into thickets, plunging through creeks,
then standing up and laughing at each other,
our faces white with thick and stinging beards—
three crazy snowmen that had come to life.

We kicked it, packed it, threw it at each other,
ate it (I still do), and if we could
get through all those layers, pissed on it:
yellow acid etching a crooked line.
But despite those blasphemies we worshiped it.
Snow! It had the power to call off school.
I never doubted that it came from heaven.

II

SKATING IN LATE AFTERNOON

As I step off the end of the dock, the dog
barks, a crack ricochets through the ice
like a vibration through a taut cable,
and I am eleven again, taking the first
tentative, gliding steps over the frozen pond.

Everyone has left. I am alone, afraid
of falling through, but soon I'm tracing
someone else's figure eight, then following
my own haphazard course over the black ice,
listening to the scraping of my skate blades.

As the sun goes down, the cedars on the hill
flare like green candle flames. They are
the dead: planted there a century ago
over victims of the plague,
by now completely taken up into their branches.

Each time I swing around toward them,
they've filled a little more with shadow,
until the last orange light breaks off the tips
into invisibility—as if their souls
were burning off so they could sleep.

Dark presences—they seem, now that I have become
aware of them, to be aware of me.

GRAVEYARD

There are children buried in this hill.

I remember my father stabbing the ground
with a fire poker, digging up gravestones.
He'd nicked a corner with the tractor
and realized that the stone table for the man
who built the house—that picnic table
for the dead—was not the only grave here.

Most of them belonged to children, babies.
I didn't understand: they weren't old enough
to know their names, to know they were alive.
Why had they been born? My father didn't know.
Then I got dizzy wondering: what if
I'd died as a child—or hadn't been born?

Here is the wrought-iron gate he dug up,
melting into the tree it leans against.
I thought it was the door to their underground
playpen, or prison—that we had let them go.
I used to see them in the treetops
through my window as I fell asleep.

SLAUGHTER COWS

A crowd of black faces, almost angry
despite their long eyelashes, moves toward me.
Numbered tags are stapled to their ears,
as if a lottery decides which ones

will die. Their noses glimmer, their nostrils
wide as the eye sockets of human skulls.
Flies land on the swirls of their foreheads
and gather at the dark pools of their eyes

to drink. The globs of dried mud in their tails
clack like wooden beads. Some of them lose
interest in me and start to walk away.
They breathe heavily, feeding, their dewlaps

swaying. I hold out a tuft of grass,
leaning against barbed wire, but they won't take it.
One climbs another's back, then falls away.
One drinks another's piss. They are full

of death. One has my death-age in its ear.

FIELD AND WOODS

Buoyed up on a swelling sea
of goldenrod and Queen Anne's lace,
the bleached well house leans
like a tugboat hauling the rusty
barn behind it. The woods beyond
are tied back neatly with the white
ropes of birch branches, but inside
the trail is overrun with brambles
and leads only to a clearing
where mushrooms bubble up
from a log half-submerged in the earth
and the rim of a wagon wheel leans
against a tree, spokes collapsing
like the helm of a shipwreck.

SNAKE HUNTING WITH MY GRANDFATHER

(Venice, Florida)

He uncoiled the length of garden hose
and pushed it down the hole, like the snakes
we were after. They had killed the terrapins
and taken over their burrow, and we
were going to flush them out and kill them.
He poured in the gasoline, pulled up the hose,
then handed me the shotgun. I waited
and peered into the wide hole, which sloped
through sand into darkness—listening for
the rattle that I'd only heard in movies.
I thought I saw it way before I saw it
moving toward me slowly in the dark,
its tongue flicking and groping like antennae.
I fired when he told me to, and blew it
back into the hole. He reached in with a stick
and pulled it out, its head a mangled stump.
"Good shot," he said. He cut the rattle off
and later put it in a glass pill bottle
labeled with my name, the date, and the snake's length—
a relic that I long ago misplaced.

MY GRANDFATHER'S PILLS

Rummaging through the garage,
I find a glass pill bottle
from Rexall Drugs, the prescription
for my grandfather and dated
3/15/69, twelve
years before he died.
"Take as directed.
Cardilate 15 mg."
Instead of pills, it's full of
hollow-nose .22 bullets.

I know that tightening
around the heart, that feeling
of going out into the woods
and shooting a tin can to shreds.

EMINENT DOMAIN

They took my grandparents' land and flooded it
to make a recreation area.
I thought I'd be able to look into the lake
and see the farm down there: the silo,
the yellow house, the shipwrecked barn,
tobacco leaves still hanging from the rafters
now swaying like seaweed.

And memory too has put it underwater,
everything wavering, obscured, a kind of
liquid night, the sunlight turned to moonlight.
I imagine my grandfather at the bottom
of that lake, waiting for my grandmother.
From down there, the wakes of speedboats
must look like jet trails. From up here,

visiting the lake on Saturday,
nothing is familiar. Water skiers
skim the surface, making it seem
like an impenetrable shell. Sunlight
flares on the waves, keeping me
from seeing into that dark world below.
And the dead don't ever come up for air.

ELEGY

AGNES SATTLER HARRISON (1904–1986)

Back in the summer jungles of Ohio,
I walked, each morning, through the woods
and fields you painted all your life,
in the visible humidity you loved—
a bluish haze, like exhaust fumes, in the trees.

And in the afternoons I visited you
in the hospital, and told you what I'd seen:
ducks on the pond, a deer, a hawk,
an indigo bunting. And I massaged your feet,
and once or twice I made you smile.

The amaryllis on your bedside table
grew from a bulb, for weeks, bending over you
more gracefully than we, keeping vigil
long after we'd gone home—
then flowered for the last week of your life.

The sunflowers out in the garden
are more like something you would paint.
They're in bloom now, hanging their heads
in the heat, or in what could be mourning,
forming a spiral pattern of hard tears.

FOR A FRIEND IN THE HOSPITAL

On the way to visit you the other day,
I passed a colony of dandelions
bunched up against the corner of a building,
and I knew you would have seen them
as persecuted weeds, exiled from the field,
huddled together under that brick wall.

I love the idea of flowers "escaping
from cultivation," as the field guides say,
and becoming wild again, but these
had come together to create
their own garden in the hard clay.
And I knew you would have loved them for that

and picked one, perhaps, drinking the sour milk
through the straw of its green stem.

POEM

Like those spider webs strung across a path,
you don't see them until you're right on them
or until it's too late and you feel one
tickling your face—it breaks, the spider
scrambles up a strand onto a leaf,
and you go on, trailing a few new gray hairs.

Then you try to look out for them and maybe
sing a song about them to yourself
so as not to forget, but eventually
the song becomes just song, your thoughts
go out into your surroundings,
and before you can do anything about it,
you've broken another web just where
the trail opens into a field of goldenrod.

III

TRADING THE ALPS FOR THE ANDES

Sometimes you meet an older person
whose vigor seems to mock your youth.
Like my grandfather—at ninety,
he still walks for miles in the woods
and dislodges boulders from the road.
Or like my great aunt Teeny, who
picked me up at the train station
in leather pants, having danced all night.
Or the Swiss woman we met in Peru
who was there to climb the highest peaks.
She'd come alone, leaving her husband
in a wheelchair by Lake Geneva.
She described the "little avalanche"
that had swept her down a mountain.
"Like swimming in a cloud," she said,
recommending the experience.
Just talking to her over dinner
was invigorating, a glimpse
of a future as bright as snowfields.
For now we'd settle for the foothills,
for alpine lakes of unreal blue,
for this firsthand account and a view
of the peaks—as jagged as chipped
obsidian, and white as it is black.

HOW THE GINKGO GOT ITS SMELL

(Sapporo, Japan)

1

By the river the other day I saw
two Japanese women hunkered down
under a ginkgo tree, on a cloud
of yellow leaves, each with a yellow
rubber glove on one hand and a pair
of chopsticks in the other. They rummaged
through the leaves, gathering the fruit.

I walked toward them clumsily, the fruit
mashing under my shoes, feeling as if
I were breaking the surface tension
of some ritual. It was then that I noticed
the sickening smell. One of them smiled
apologetically, then showed me
how the seed squirted from the flesh.

2

Not quite as naturally as leaves,
the scraps of paper shiver on the tree.
They are fortunes the people have bought
at the shrine—bad ones, that must be tied
to the tree so that they won't come true.
They are poems about how their lives have
gone wrong. It is a process of revision.

What can be done with such ominous
prophecies? The tree makes of them a fruit
that stinks, but whose kernel resembles
an almond and is delicious when baked.
When the leaves swarm like yellow butterflies,
the fruit hang from the branches like cocoons
full of promises for the coming year.

TEACHING PREP SCHOOL

On my way to the airport for the interview,
the sun came up over the trees
like a giant yellow traffic light,
cautioning me, I realized even then,
not to take the job.
But six months later there I was
facing a classroom full of rowdy kids
in an old manor house that stood
like a white ship on top of a hill,
the halyards slapping against the flagpole.
"Man overboard!" I used to joke to myself,
trying to pretend I wasn't miserable.
Or: "The captain is a drunk." He kept
an icebox in his office full of Heinekens
and guzzled them while looking through binoculars
at the girls' soccer team stretching out
on the dusty playing field. Once, at a party,
I listened to him gurgle drunkenly
about how the blacks had ruined America.
Then he belched his insults
at people in the room, including me.
Everyone seemed to think it was funny.
I felt awkward, like a stray cornstalk
in a field of soybeans, so I sat down
and stared into my glass
as through the wrong end of a telescope—
I wanted to be that far away.
My plaid shirt underneath the glass
turned into fields seen from the window
of an airplane. I had already left,
and, realizing this, I was suddenly happy.

THE MODEL HOUSE

Three weeks after moving into an apartment
in a building that's under renovation,
you bring a building into the apartment—
or what will be a building, but is now
just scattered pieces, drawings, and frustration.
It's actually a house, which you designed
and now are building brick by tiny brick.
You've brought this thing into our lives, thrust it
between us. It's all I've heard about for weeks.

Meanwhile, the apartment's still unfinished:
the walls sprout tentacles of wire, the roof leaks,
the oven won't go on. Workers barge in
all day, tracking sawdust footprints, hammering,
and grinding cigarettes into the floor.
And outside they're tearing up the street.
But still you have to make it worse each night
by bringing this construction site indoors:
buckets of plaster, piles of wooden bricks
(all that's missing are the Tonka trucks).

You sit there in the middle of that mess,
gluing it together with tears. It's 2 A.M.
I try to help, but soon I'm raving, shaking
my arms above it like an angry god
who could smash it to bits at any moment.
You push me away. I go to bed, thinking:
This again, another year of architecture school—
your second. And our sixth year of marriage.
Then I remember: you were the only one
of all the married students in your class
whose marriage held together that first year.

A house is meant to make you feel at home,
but this one's doing just the opposite.
If we could only live out in the country
things would be better. Then you could design
apartments in the city, like our own. . . .
A little later, I'm on the floor again
sawing curved pieces with a coping saw,
gluing, fitting walls together, and thinking
(now that the thing is almost finished):
Someday we may live in a house like this.

ELEGY FOR THE CLOTHESLINES

No laundry flutters in the wind today.
No bright towels or underwear festoons
our lives, and no sheets billow like loose sails.
No one leans out the windows, gathering in
bundles of sun-warmed clothes with which we might
renew ourselves. Only the dingy air
hangs between the houses, under a sky
permeated with the lint of smog.

The clotheslines that once crisscrossed these backyards
are mostly gone. The gadgetry that used to
lift our clothes into the sky like kites
has broken down: now the tall poles lean,
their pulleys rusty and their rungs askew.
These abandoned ladders to the sky,
only the ivy climbs them now. But night
slides down them still into the neighborhood.

REFLECTION ON THE VIETNAM WAR
MEMORIAL

Here it is, the back porch of the dead.
You can see them milling around in there,
    screened in by their own names,
    looking at us in the same
vague and serious way we look at them.

An underground house, a roof of grass—
one version of the underworld. It's all
    we know of death: a world
    like our own (but darker, blurred),
inhabited by beings like ourselves.

The location of the name you're looking for
can be looked up in a book whose resemblance
    to a phone book seems to claim
    some contact can be made
through the simple act of finding a name.

As we touch the name the stone absorbs our grief.
It takes us in—we see ourselves inside it.
    And yet we feel it as a wall
    and realize the dead are all
just names now, the separation final.

THE LIGHT CURE

It doesn't matter where you are.
You will find it, when you need it,
at the end of day, in the intricate
flames of leafless trees, or the last light
climbing up a row of brownstones, getting
yellower, more tangible, but further,
until the cornices alone are glowing;
their chipped paint and ragged nests become
a glorious decay, the rich detail
of magical roofs above our drab world.
Even the matted feathers of the starlings
shine like birds of paradise. Crane your neck
for that moment when the light snaps
upward, the earth is buried, and everything
that matters dissolves into the sky,
because something in you may be lifted
or slightly pulled askew, as your body sinks.

IN SAINT JOHN THE DIVINE

This cathedral is a skeleton of stone.
What is the flesh? Someone truly faithful
might say faith—or God himself.
I remember a letter from a friend
describing the rising voices of the choir
filling up the church he'd visited
and brimming over among shafts of light
slanting through the clerestory windows.

Here, a smoky vapor in the vaulting
is crisscrossed by the beams of floodlights,
and I remember the same friend's bitter comment
after leaving the seminary:
"They don't believe in God, they believe in smoke."
If that haze among those bending triangles
is God, then he's a dark god, too diffuse
for me to comprehend. I leave, thinking:

My faith is less complete than this cathedral,
whose jamb figures are uncarved blocks,
whose transept is unvaulted—its plain dome
looks like a planetarium—and whose
invisible spires are circled by pigeons.
Mine is the religion of ruined abbeys:
naves carpeted with grass and striped with shadows—
open to the sky, clouds racing over.

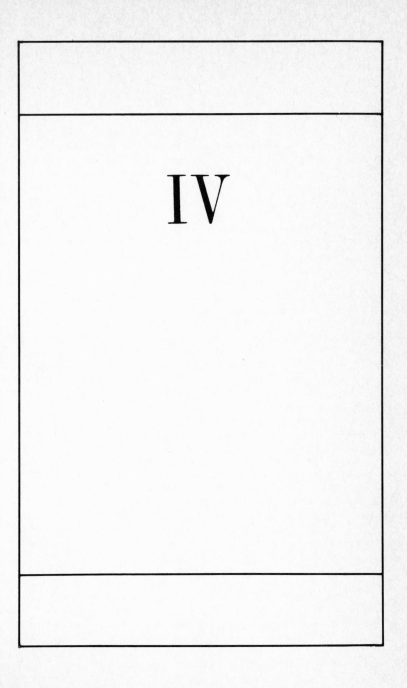

IV

DISCOVERIES UNDER TREES

Buddha under the bo tree,
Augustine under the fig tree,
Newton under the apple tree—
the discoveries become more
limited: wisdom, faith, knowledge.
What comes next, in our time? Nothing
but a sense of things as they are,
and that's enough for me, right now
at least, under this birch
whose copper trunk arches one way
then changes its mind, doubles back,
and sweeps up into a cloud
of leaves, yellow blended with green.
There is a waterfall nearby,
but if I threw an empty bowl
into it, it would not float
upstream. Nor did I fling myself
under this tree, weeping, to be
enlightened by the voice of
a child. And I'm not fasting
to deepen my meditation
on telescopes. I'm just sitting.

BATHTUBS, THREE VARIETIES

First the old-fashioned kind, standing on paws,
like a domesticated animal—
I once had a whole flock of these
(seven—for good luck? I never asked
the landlord) under a walnut tree
in my backyard, like sheep in shade.
They collected walnuts in the fall
then filled up with snow, like thickening wool.

Modern tubs are more like ancient tombs.
And it is a kind of death we ask for
in the bath. Nothing theatrical
like Marat with his arm hanging out—
just that the boundary between the body
and the world dissolves, that we forget
ourselves, and that the tub becomes
the sarcophagus of dreams.

My bathtub in Japan was square, and deep.
You sat cross-legged like a Zen
monk in meditation, up to your neck
in water always a little too hot,
relaxed and yet attentive to the moment
(relaxation as a discipline)—
staring through a rising cloud of steam
at the blank wall in front of you.

BUTTERFLIES

The rest stops along the highway
are repetitions in a dream.
Time feels strange to us. We don't know
if it's morning or afternoon.
We drink the rusty water, stretch
our legs, eat at a picnic table,
then return to the blue Plymouth.
It is then that we notice them:
butterflies, flattened on the grille
as if a lepidopterist
had pinned them there. It is
a nice collection: two monarchs,
three small yellow ones, and a black
and yellow swallowtail with two
blue spots. Others are crumpled, torn
(like fragments of an image
inside a kaleidoscope),
or smashed into the radiator.
The car is like a whale that feeds
by sifting shrimp through its baleen
as it cruises on "the whale-road."
And like a whale it doesn't think
it shouldn't kill. It doesn't think
at all—we do. We think: *How
beautiful, this death*.
I try to peel one off
and burn my fingers.

RETURNING TO CUTTYHUNK

I've heard half a dozen meanings for the name
and none of them alike. To me it always seemed
a baby's nickname for a baby island:
a low, scruffy hill on the horizon,
so small it looks as if the windmill on it
might lift it off the ocean like a seaplane.

That day the Sunday *Globe* said it meant "Go away,"
and I believed it. I thought they must have turned
the windmill on like an electric fan,
a wind machine that blew the whitecaps off
the green reptilian waves, into our faces.
We gave up and tacked into Sakonnet.

After the storm blew over, we tried again.
We spotted Cuttyhunk. At first the cliffs
of Gay Head looked like part of it. The windmill
stood there in the middle, without waving
its arms, and stared at us inscrutably.
The Gosnold monument was over to the right,

like a lonely chess rook in its corner
waiting for the most strategic moment
to castle with the windmill-king.
The harbor on the other side looked like
a plate full of hors d'oeuvres, bristling with toothpicks.
Then we saw the gray, Monopoly-sized houses.

When we sailed past tiny, treeless Penikese
(a former leper colony and now
a bird sanctuary), the waves were so smooth—
more like a lake's than an ocean's—it was
as if the thinnest film of mist were on them,
softening the blues and oranges of sunset.

We docked near the fish shacks, then walked up the road
between two blooming hedges: the island
took us in its arms (privet, milkweed,
honeysuckle, multiflora rose).
The evening air seemed hazy from the pollen.
I said, "It's happening, the island's taking off."

We walked along a dry stone wall with orange
lichen on it, like spilled paint, dried and cracked,
and past a little church whose weather vane
was a striped bass, wide-eyed and open-mouthed
as if astonished by the clouds above him
which looked like pink cabbages in a blue field.

SCALLOP

FOR CHARLIE WORTHEN

Eons ahead
of the sedentary clam,
the scallop can fly,
however gimpily,
underwater, snapping away, all mouth,
like castanets that have escaped
a dancer's hand—

only to be caught
again by ours:
you picked one up, took off
your mask and snorkle
to better see the tiny eyes
that cling like bubbles to the rim
(minuscule blue pearls)

and the fringe
of filaments, revealed,
like hundreds of snail horns,
as the mollusk
slowly opened up—
then it snapped shut, squirting you
in the eye like a trick rose.

All afternoon
we chased them
so we could eat the soft
cylindrical
white muscle
which makes possible
their flight, our pleasure.

THE PEACOCK FLOUNDER

(The New England Aquarium)

They say flounders are camouflaged
to blend in with the bottom of the ocean,
but that can't be true for this one
unless the bottom where he comes from
is covered with Persian rugs.
The aquarium is not: maybe that's why
he doesn't deign to swim down there.
He ripples slowly like a flying carpet,
opening and closing his sideways mouth.

Now and then he swims up to the top
and breaks the mirror surface with bulging,
limpetlike eyes, as if he had to
take in the view above the tank
as a whale or dolphin takes in air.
He almost has the whole tank to himself:
the four or five other fish are not
colorful, and they're so thin that when
they turn toward us they disappear.

With what effort did his eyes push
around to one side, concentrating
a million years of evolution
into a few weeks? And how are we
to understand him if not by a like
effort of the eyes?—feeling our gaze
pulled askance by his, our mouths twisting
until we realize that we, after all,
are secretly disturbed about our lives.

THE MUTE SWAN

(Cygnus olor)

Now it seems more than mere coincidence
that the sinuous neck of the swan looks
like a snake about to strike and that
the black bulb on its forehead makes it seem
slightly deranged—now, that is, that a man
has been dredged up from the bottom of the lake.

His boat was found empty, nosing into shore
with the motor still droning. His cigarettes
and hat were floating nearby. Nobody
heard a cry, only splashing, and then the swan
was seen swimming away with its beak
in the air and its wings up like sails.

THE OTTER IN THE WASHINGTON ZOO

is in love with a little girl.
Maybe it's because he's been
alone too long—or is it just
her red shirt he's attracted to?

She runs from one end to the other
of his window, and he follows,
swimming undulously, bubbles
trailing along his slick body.

She stops in the middle, and he
swerves to a halt, floating upright
with only his head above the water.
They are about the same size.

They stare into each other's eyes.
Then she ducks down, and he
dives to the bottom of the pool.
She is laughing and he is laughing bubbles.

The glass becomes a kind of mirror:
he returns her every movement with
a replica more graceful and alluring
to make her stay—leading her on

by following her lead. But now
her mother says it's time to go,
and she leaves him looking after her,
pawing lightly at the wall of glass.

SWIMMING LESSONS

(Harbor Seals, Point Reyes)

They could be driftwood from this far above,
strewn on that crescent of beach at the cliff's base,
bleached gray. Except that now and then they move:
a pup and mother bounce until they reach
the water, and flop in. Then we see other
swerving forms—each pup clinging to its mother
or swimming alongside, or playing chase,
until a breaker rolls them up the beach.

We watch and watch, but it's never long enough.
And our binoculars aren't strong enough:
we want to be *among* them in the surf,
swimming through kelp—that would be happiness.
No matter when it comes, our leaving is
an interruption, like the cliff between us.

SWIMMING AT NEAP TIDE

(Wareham, Massachusetts)

The water was so shallow
we had to lie down in beds
of seaweed, mattresses of murk,
pillowed by harmless jellyfish.

We dreamed we were whales, humming
underwater, then breaching
again and again, until the smack
of waves finally woke us.

Then we walked like crabs to shore
where we stood upright, becoming
human again, heavy again
with all our human concerns.

V

Bisby Lake Poems

ARRIVAL AT THE CABIN

After ten miles on a dusty road,
the driveway is a kind of car wash:
a strip of tall grass in the middle
brushes underneath, the dense ferns, leaning
inward, wipe the sides, and a low spruce branch
scrapes along the roof, squeaking a little.

The smell of ferns, pine, and mint gives way,
when we open the cabin door, to mothballs.
We clean up, put out the Indian rugs,
take down the poles that hold the roof up
under winter snows. By that time it's dark,
and we set out with towels and flashlights.

It's the Fourth of July. No fireworks, just
a little lightning—silent, but it lights up
the whole lake for eerie, trembling moments
as bright as day but a cold blue. Your body
is white, knee-deep in the black water,
the bubbles phosphorescent when you dive.

FIRST DAY AT THE LAKE

I wake up early. Patches of cold night
still cling to the corners of the room,
under the dresser and bed. My breath clouds.
Then I look out the window and see
a scene that could be from a dream:
the lake is piled so high with mist
and lit so brightly by the sun
it looks like a cloud seen from above.
I get up and hurry into my clothes,
taking the change out of my pockets
so as not to frighten the animals.
Outside, the roofs are steaming.
I hear a quiet splashing from the lake
and see, through the trees, a doe and fawn
wading in the shallow water, drinking.
Ripples spread around them, making the sunlight
quiver brightly under the sliding mist.
Three mergansers swim right by them,
and neither duck nor deer fears the other.
I stay hidden in the trees, removed.
When they lift their heads to listen,
sunlight spills from their mouths.

NEWTS

Lolling on the dock in the afternoon sunlight
of late May in the Adirondacks,
we notice two newts lolling
in the shallow water under us. But not
just lolling: they are entwined in sex,
the male lightly clasping the female's neck,
their tails entangled and their tiny eyes
vacant, as if half asleep with pleasure.

Then we spot others, dozens, and excitedly
pick them out from the bottom's
sand and sticks and leaf rot: olive green
with red spots outlined in black, some of them
twisted so we can see their yellow bellies
speckled with black—and all of them
coupled into double salamanders, their tails
curled in a calligraphy of pleasure.

They are almost motionless, except
for an occasional ripple through a tail.
Then one pair begins to writhe,
squirming and thrashing in what looks like pain,
until the female wriggles free and they both rest.
We could catch one, as we often have
in August, but we know
we're privileged to have chanced upon this scene.

So we leave them alone, and they are caught
only in the undulant, unraveling
net of yellow light the waves
pull along the bottom—a watery fire.
Their offspring will be orange flames

scurrying through bunchberry and wintergreen
until they feel the change come over them,
the memory of water pulling them

back to this lake where they'll twist themselves
into these ribbons, these love knots.

FOXGLOVE

Like fishmouths, the lower lip
protruding, the flowers open up
to take their one long breath,
and again the burly bumblebees
muscle their way into the caves
where their sweet, secret
rite takes place. Spires, bells,
spires of bells, it is the bees'
religion. Inside, the script
of desire—pink
freckles, the fine hair
of a girl's cheek, the curves
of stamens, like elaborate tusks—
draws them in. They stumble out
like drunken sailors, their forearms
heavy with nectar, pollen
stuck to their fuzz
like beer froth on a beard.

A FIELD GUIDE TO MOSSES

I'd love to assemble a compendium of mosses
in which the mosses were actually growing.
All the different textures and shades of green
would be right there on the thick damp pages:
the tentacled, the shaggy wool, the smooth-as-velvet.
All kinds of lichen would also be included:
rust-orange, acid-yellow, copper oxide-green,
and the red-tipped nodes known as British soldiers.
And maybe some fungi fringing the pages.

It would be a large work, several volumes,
two or three feet of shelf space, and the shelf
would be out in the woods somewhere, between two trees.
Instead of silverfish or bookworms in the bindings
there would be salamanders, wriggling away
whenever you opened the waterlogged covers.
But eventually the shelf would rot and collapse,
and the tomes would lie like rotting logs, covered with moss,
and slowly sink into the ground forever.

ADIRONDACKS: EARTH AND SKY

Each year the cabins sink deeper.
The ground will accept anything; it gives
under our feet, reminding us
that someday it will take our bodies.
But now it gives back as much as it takes:
moss, ferns, mushrooms, wintergreen,
bunchberry, foxglove, hemlock, spruce.

But the sky's gifts, those gifts we can't
possess, but only see, are vaster.
Taking only our breath, it gives us the pink
sunset and blue air of evening, the stars'
rich loam, and sometimes the northern lights
rising like steam, in feathery streaks,
or swimming like fish through the stars.

At the age of three I was woken up,
brought into the courtyard with the well
in the middle and the blue globes
of thistles around the edge—and still
half asleep, told to look at the sky.
My mother said the word *rainbow*.
The sky's gifts are like that: part of a rite.

THE NEW GEOGRAPHY

As we drift on the lake, the world ends
just beyond those hills surrounding it.
The lake floats in space, it is so quiet.
No sound but the dripping of our paddles.

But then we hear the thunder, scraping
and apocalyptic whistling of two
army-green jets that rocket over us,
dragging all of history behind them.

This chain of lakes must flash up at them,
breathtaking but irrelevant to chains
of events, and chain reactions inside
the furious secrets they are loaded with.

What can we do? We make sandwiches
and walk to our favorite picnic rock.
The lichen on it looks like a map,
a new, desolate geography.

CANOEING IN THE RAIN

A fine rain hisses on the lake's surface
and gusts blow big drops off the trees
as I paddle along the shore.
I see a bullfrog
white belly up among the reeds.

I turn it over with my paddle, and find
no green at all, just faded brown
like an old mushroom.
And hanging from its gaping mouth
the wet tattered rags of its guts.

I've hardly heard them sing at all this year.
So much like a drowned man, its legs
and arms outstretched. The rain
sprinkles its hissing acid on the lake
and a light mist rises like fumes.

CLEAR DAY

North wind today, the lake
rolls its thalo blue toward us
in steady waves and darker,
fanning gusts. The only
decisive wind we have, it
cleans up the sky, sweeps out
yesterday's clouds like clumps
of dust, and makes everything
crisp in its outline, just a bit
more real.

On hazy days,
the lake is a pale gray, just
like the sky, and the mountains
on the far shore, no longer
green but darker gray,
look like a strip of clouds,
as if the only view, framed
by hemlocks (moving their arms
slowly like underwater
plants), were sky.

Today,
the lake is just the lake (or
more the lake than ever, bluer),
the mountains are themselves
again, and the hemlocks are
gesticulating wildly
as if exhilarated by this
unambiguous view. Life
is seldom this clear, free
of illusions, even here
where we come to get away.

THE ONE THAT GOT AWAY

FOR JULIE

We paddled through the winding waterway,
past lily pads and water hyacinths,
into the other lake: perfectly calm
and of a blue much deeper than usual.
It was that time of day when late sunlight
intensifies the beauty of everything,
transforming the trees into a green fire.
They leaned over us as we paddled by
as if with the desire to be draped
in undulating nets of yellow light
projected by the waves from our canoe—
waves in which those very trees were mirrored,
stretched and wavering. We drifted in silence.
The paddle that I held across my lap
dripped, as if to count the passing moments—
getting slower, but we knew they wouldn't stop.
And we knew those nets of light, unraveling
all the while, wouldn't catch the afternoon
for us to keep—though you turned to me and said
that this was all you wanted in the world.

NOTES

"Bathtubs, Three Varieties." "Marat with his arm hanging out" refers
to Jacques Louis David's painting *The Death of Marat* (1793).

"The Peacock Flounder." "With what effort . . . a few weeks?" Young
flounders look like most other fish, with an eye on each side of
their heads. As they develop, one eye migrates to the other side,
encapsulating the evolutionary process by which they became
flatfish.

"The Mute Swan." This poem is based on a newspaper story.